103 Proven Sales Tips

The Professionals Guide to Higher Income

Justin Hammonds

Inspire Publications
A Division of
Inspire Consultants

For information about special discounts for bulk purchases, please contact:
info@JustinHammonds.com

Inspire Consultants can bring this author to your live event. For more information or to book an event contact:
info@JustinHammonds.com

Cover Photo by Nathan Mantor Photography
Nathanmantorphotography.com
ISBN-10:0615501249
ISBN-13:978-0615501246

DEDICATION

This book is dedicated to the men and women who make the economy move.
The SALES FORCE!

Acknowledgments

I would like to thank the sales professionals that I have had the opportunity to learn from and the sales teams that I have been blessed to lead and develop. It's been an honor sharing in your success.

Thank you to my coaches Zig Ziglar, Brendon Burchard, Brian Tracy and John Maxwell for all the advice and wisdom they have shared over the years.

To my wife and children: Being your husband and father is the greatest honor I could ever have.

To my Lord and Savior, Jesus Christ: I thank you for your grace and mercy. To you may the glory be.

Matthew 10:32

Table of Contents

Introduction

This book is intended to be used as a practical guide for the sales professional. Regardless of the product, the price point, or the client, this book will serve you well.

The tips contained within this book would take decades of selling experience to acquire. They are presented here in an easy to understand format that allows you to accelerate your sales career at a pace that will amaze you.

Think of these tips as advice not a fancy dissertation on the art of selling. This is not another long and boring "how-to guide" that most seasoned professionals dread. This book was written purposely in short points so the time invested will be minimal while the return will be great.

If you are looking for proven sales techniques, strategies, and tactics that will allow you to reach levels of production that has evaded you in the past, then read on. Take notes and develop these tips to make them relate to your specific market. I challenge you to immediately put into motion as many of these tips as you can. The time for action is now!

I encourage you to embrace your sales career and become one of the top earners in the industry. You can do it and this book will help you reach your sales goals!

"There is no security in life, only opportunity."

-Mark Twain

Tip #1

Open the deal!

Strike the industry phrase of closing the deal and replace it with opening the deal. The idea that you closed the deal has led to poor client service. When you make the sale you have just opened the deal. You have opened the relationship to continued client service and more sales! Begin conditioning your thoughts to think of the long term relationship and multiple sales. You do that by opening the deal not closing it.

Tip #2

Have a healthy view of self.

Nothing will hold you back more than yourself. Having a healthy view of yourself will increase your confidence. People love to do business with confident people. Make yourself as attractive to business as possible and start today to view yourself as the success that you are.

Tip #3

View yourself as a professional regardless of what you sell.

It doesn't matter if you sell fish at a pet store or multimillion dollar products. View yourself as a professional and act as one. Your product does not determine if you are a professional, it's your actions, thoughts, and the way you conduct your business.

Tip #4

Understand the unique opportunity a sales career provides.

A sales career will provide you the ability to earn what you are worth. Most sales positions will pay you in accordance with the value you bring to the organization. How many other careers will pay you based on the value you bring? Most will pay you based upon what the value the position brings not the person filling it. A sales career is truly only limited by you.

When you set your sights on becoming a professional sales person, you will enjoy more time freedom than 95 percent of the working class. How fast you become a professional is determined by you.

Tip #5

View sales as a career not just a job.

Part of the ability to make the leap from a sales person to a sales professional is how you view sales. If your thought is that this is just a job then you will have a difficult time taking the steps necessary to become a true professional.

The difference between a job and a career is the perceived value you place on it. How much self development are you willing to do for a job? How much self development are you willing to do for a career? When you begin to make a mental shift from job, to career, you begin to view the process in a different way. It's in this shift that you will begin to see your sales increase as your skill level develops.

Tip #6

Learn how to sell.

There is no substitute for learning the fundamentals of selling. Once you have done that you will never be out of work. This gives you freedom to align your selling career with your purpose and passion. Everything we touch has been sold. When you learn the fundamentals of selling you will be able to take those skills to whatever market you like. The key is…learn how to sell!

Tip #7

Invest in your sales career with professional coaching.

Having the ability to sell constantly requires skill. Typically these skills are learned through trial and error of personal experience. It's this approach to learning that causes many sales people to never make the money they deserve or experience the freedom they desire. Learning from personal experience is valuable, however learning form other peoples experience is more valuable. The reason is simple, it costs you less. You spend less in money, in time, in effort, and missed opportunities. If you want to accelerate your career, invest in learning from the best.

There are people who have been blessed with a natural ability to sell. Those natural abilities need to be refined if they are to take their sales to a new level. Do that by taking the time to learn the fundamentals and advanced skills from experts.

Study-at-home courses and workshops can accelerate your career faster than any one other thing. Professionals from every industry have coaches. Professional athletes to successful business people all invest in coaching. Why should you be different?

Books and C.D.'s have a minimal investment with a huge upside; I encourage you to get a coach. Whether it's virtual or physical, learn from the best. It will be one of the wisest investments that you will ever make.

Tip #8

Stress vs. Pressure

Stress is bred from not being prepared. Stress is a negative feeling that produces negative energy. One should avoid stress in all areas of their life. Pressure is something entirely different. Pressure is born out of an opportunity to advance your current situation. Perhaps it is the opportunity to advance your career with a potential large client. Regardless of what it is when you feel pressure embrace it. Fully embrace the opportunity that is being presented to you with the preparedness of a professional.

Tip #9

Understand that it is the benefits that sell.

It's not what the product is; it's what the product does! Understand the benefits behind the product or service. If you sell washing machines "what the product is" is a washer. If you sell the benefit it's the fact that this washer will wash more clothes at one time than others thus reducing the time it takes to do the laundry by two hours a week. What would you do with an extra two hours a week? This is the benefit. All washing machines wash clothes, not all washing machines wash clothes and create time. Find the benefit for your product or service and develop it into a powerful presentation.

Tip #10

Your product or service must solve a problem, satisfy a need, want, or desire to be viable.

Understand where your product fits and how it accomplishes its purpose. If you can't position your product to solve a problem, satisfy a need, want, or desire then you have no viable product. It is imperative that you understand which category or multiple categories your product fills so you can position it properly.

Tip #11

Always operate from a position of an expert.

Operating from the power position as an expert allows you to build trust faster and helps relieve the client's natural reluctances of making the purchase. Seek to position yourself as an expert in your industry and you will have clients seeking you out to do business.

Tip #12

Understand and practice the consultant sales model.

In the consultant sales model you are acting as a trusted adviser. You are advising your client of their options and giving them your professional opinion as it pertains to that particular situation. You are counseling the client on how to proceed. Rather than "selling" the client. It is important to remember that you are on the same team looking for a team win.

Tip #13

Do nothing to a client. Do it for your client.

Years ago the sales profession earned a bad reputation by producing a generation of "Do it to you" sales people. They used hard pressure and at times underhanded tactics to sell their goods. Some years ago a new revolution in sales occurred ushered in by the great sales developer Zig Ziglar. Teaching his method of sales has raised the standards for all in the profession today. You only win when your client wins. No one wins using cheap tactics and misstatements. In the words of Zig Ziglar himself, "People don't care how much you know till they know how much you care." You do that by helping them and serving them. Brendon Burchard the founder of *Experts Academy* has built a very successful business based upon the principle of "adding value to your clients." These are great pieces of advice to keep in focus, adding value and demonstrating your genuine concern for your clients is a winning strategy.

Tip #14

Never take shortcuts.

There is no such thing as a short cut in sales. In the long run it will take you longer and will always cost you more. So take the time it takes and you will find that it takes less time. You will profit more and your client will appreciate the world class service.

Tip #15

Be yourself. Never imitate others.

This is an urge that many new sales people find hard to fight. When they see others that are being successful they immediately began to imitate them. This is unwise. You should learn from them, study their habits and techniques to see how you can develop them in yourself. The key is to develop them not to imitate them. Be yourself, develop your skill set, and leave the imitation to others.

Tip #16

Invest your time with successful people.

Regardless of what they are successful in, being around successful people helps you become successful. Learn the way they think, their behaviors, and their thought patterns. This exposure will serve as a platform for you to grow and develop those same traits. You might start to realize that some of your thoughts were holding you back. Remember success breeds more success.

Tip #17

Become a sponge for new information.

Strive to learn as much as you can from as many people as you can. View yourself as a sponge soaking up as much information as your brain will allow. Information has the power to change your life when you put it into action. Don't be a collector of information become an applicator of it. It can be one thought or idea that changes your life forever. Keep an open and objective mind that is always searching for new ways to learn.

Tip #18

View yourself as a marketer.

Sales is more about marketing than it is about selling. One of the mistakes that a lot of new and experienced sales people make is viewing themselves as sales people. The reality is that you are a marketer. You are marketing your products and services. When you start to view yourself as a marketer you begin to look at ways to effectively get your message out to the right people. Getting the message to the correct people makes the sales process much easier.

Marketing, as I view it, is anything you do that positively promotes you and your business. Marketing encompasses a wide spectrum of activities. From T.V., radio, print, articles, public speaking, networking, social media, internet blogging; the list is endless. Many of these activities cost very little; think about your industry and how you can begin your marketing activities.

Tip #19

Stop prospecting and start marketing.

For years in the sales world we have been told we must prospect for new business. This statement is true, we need to always be looking to develop new business. However words create powerful images that lodge in our subconscious mind and produce feelings. I have attempted to strike the word prospecting from my vocabulary. For me, when I hear the word prospecting I think of an old man wandering around the hills aimlessly turning over rock after rock looking for gold. Once the rock is turned over and nothing is found he moves on never thinking about it again. The prospector is operating on the premise that if he can find his lucky strike then he will be rich quick. Do you know sales people like that? I do. I have seen them go from one prospect to the other looking for the quick and easy sale. When they strike a little gold they ravage the client for as much as they possibly can and never think about follow up client service because they are content with the initial sale. They leave their clients feeling like an old mine; stripped and abandoned. Obviously this is not going to produce referrals, repeat business, or any positive feelings for you or your company.

The marketer realizes that there are four key points to consider when developing new business.

1.   Information Overload:

Today more than ever people are overloaded with information. They will only give a small amount of their attention to your message. Because of that fact you must be sure it is clear and adds value.

2.   Multiple Touches are Required:

Because of the fact that people are bombarded with information and stimulus we generally need to touch/make contact with our future clients multiple times for our message to reach them. Each touch/contact should be designed to build credibility and trust.

3.   Credibility and Trust:

The more times our future client sees or hears our message the more credible they perceive us. Touching/making contact in a professional way from the position of an expert allows them to begin to develop trust. This makes it easier for them to move the relationship further into the sale.

4.   **Timing:**

We must consistently stay in front of our future clients with our marketing message. Timing is a part of the equation as it pertains to selling. Remember clients buy when the time is right for them, not always when you want them to. When the time is right for them you need to be in the proper position to open the deal. You do that by staying in front of your future clients with a well thought out and planned series of marketing touches.

As you have noticed I have used the word "touch" as a replacement for making contact. I'm not implying that you physically touch your future clients. What I am saying is that you make each contact personal and with the clear purpose of build credibility and trust. Often times we view contacting our future clients with a single purpose of making the sale right then. It is this mentality that handicaps your sales career.

As you move from the prospector to the marketer you see that every rock has the potential to deliver gold at some point. The key is to turn over a lot of rocks but go back to those rocks and turn them over multiple times. Just because you don't see gold the first time you turn it over doesn't mean it isn't there. Keep marketing, keep digging around a little deeper and you may find that the timing is right and the gold was just under the surface.

Tip #20

Network.

Any sales professional will tell you networking can be extremely rewarding if done properly. They will also tell you it is a waste of time if you don't have a plan and purpose to follow.

When networking at an event view it from the other person's perspective. You must be aware that everyone at a networking event is there with the same agenda, to create business. However, few know the proper approach. Most will hand you a card and tell you what they do and move on to someone else. The hope is that you will happen to keep their card forever and call or refer them if you need a service they provide. But what does a card really tell you? A much better tactic is to ask the other person what their ideal client looks like and share with them what your ideal client looks like. Be interested in what they need so that they will become interested in your needs. If possible throughout the event find a person that might fit their ideal client list and make an introduction. They both will be appreciative and you will have successfully connected with two people who will in turn be on the lookout for your ideal client.

In order for networking to be successful you must identify the people who would be the most beneficial to your business and focus your attention on working with them. Having 200 business cards of people who have no influence in your market is not the best strategy to use. Remember to be engaging and find ways to connect others together and they will become connectors for you.

Tip #21

Price, Protection, Service or Knowledge?

Most products have a combination of these elements. Which is more important to your clients? Which area do you excel in? You must know the answer to these questions.

For example look at the dynamics when shopping for a vehicle. What do you think is the most important factor for a mother of three children? Protection, she will want to know that the vehicle will protect her family if they are ever involved in a crash. The 21 year old that is purchasing their first car would most likely be looking at price. Perhaps the elderly couple wants to know that they will always have the best service if they have an issue. It's the savvy client that is looking for the knowledge to ensure that they are getting the right vehicle for their needs.

Don't be afraid to ask your client which is more important to them. This is a great question that generally stimulates the conversation.

Knowledge is a specialty item and is the key factor in "how to" products and services. Receiving access to an expert in a particular field can significantly increase the value of the product or service. This is just one of the many reasons that you should position yourself as an expert (Tip #11).

Tip #22

Access and Influence

If you're going to sell to someone you must have access to them. We would all agree it is very difficult to sell without access. When you first start your sales career you are encouraged to go to your warm market. The reason is simple, you have access to those people. It is more difficult to gain access to people that you have no connection with. How do you get access? Typically access and influence are associated with each other. When you have influence with someone, typically you can gain access. There are degrees and levels of influence, how much influence you need to gain access to the people you want to see will depend upon who your client is. Obviously to gain access to the C.E.O. of a Fortune 500 company you will need more influence than that of a smaller organization.

Gain influence for a sales situation can be accomplished with marketing. Our marketing efforts can be broken down into two categories; TIME or MONEY. When I first began my sales career I had more time than I had money (sound familiar?) so I personally had to do all of my marketing. I created my own brochures; I scheduled my own appointments and performed all of my own future client touches (industry refers to them as cold calls). As my business grew so did the money. It grew to the point that money was a larger resource than my time. So I began to make the shift and eventually hired fifteen marketers to perform aspects of my marketing plan that I no longer had the time myself to do.

Remember that you must have access to create a sale. In most cases influence, to some degree, will be involved in the creation of the initial access. So think of access and influence as a pair and attempt to establish them with as many people as you can.

Tip #23

Strike the word customer from your vocabulary and replace it with Client.

Girlfriend or Wife? Which one implies a deeper level of commitment? This is the same principle when we make the distinction between customers or clients. Customer implies a much more casual relationship while a client implies a commitment. When you refer to those who buy from you as your client you subconsciously are telling them that they are valued and you are committed to their needs. These statements also reinforce your commitment to that level of service. Treat them like clients; refer to them as clients and you will be amazed at how your clients will refer other clients to you.

Tip #24

Know your sales cycle.

The sales cycle is how long and the steps necessary to move your client from the first touch to the opening of the sale and through the delivery of goods or services. Without understanding the cycle you will never be able to run your sales career like a business. Some industries have many variables to their cycle but typically there are definable patterns that must take place. Know what they are and understand what you need to do to ensure that your client moves through each of them smoothly.

Tip #25

Track your sales cycle with all clients.

It is not enough to just know the sales cycle you must track your clients through the sales cycle. This is an extremely effective tool that allows you to accurately forecast your sales. The professional understands the importance of being able to track their clients through the sales cycle looking for anything that is out of the ordinary that could cause the progression to slow. Being alert allows you to address any issue that may potentially cost you the sale. This is particularly useful if your market requires multiple team members working together to complete the transaction.

 If for some reason your client fails to complete the sales cycle make notes so that you will be aware of the situation the next time you enter the cycle with them. This way you can pay special attention to that area.

Tip #26

Establish a Goal Reaching Program.

Many sales professionals and organizations fail to understand the power of a proper goal reaching system. In fact the majority of people know little about goals and what they have been taught is not always fundamentally sound.

Most of us have been told to "set" goals and then work hard to achieve them and that is as far as it goes. This is not enough. Setting goals is the easy part, if you want to accelerate your success, you must have a system that works on your subconscious, your conscience, and involves measurable strategic action.

I have spent more than twenty-five years studying and applying the best practices I have learned about goals. I have compiled all that I have learned into the Purposed, Healthy and Determined Goal Reaching System (P.H.D.) that is outlined here. This system has proven to be powerful and effective. This system, if followed, is guaranteed to bring you personal success in all areas of your life. It's not merely enough to write it, as is the case in most goal setting programs. The P.H.D. Goal Reaching System is founded on action. It's about high-yield, measurable action and accelerating the speed with which your goals are reached. The system is comprised of five stages, and each stage builds on the other.

Stage One
- **Identify the Goal**

The goal must be realistic and specific. It must also be identifiable as well as measurable.

Stage Two
- **List the Costs**

What will you have to sacrifice to reach the goal? There will always be a sacrifice to make. Are you willing to pay the cost?

Stage Three
- **Writing the Goal**

Once we write the goal, it starts to become reality. Up until this point, it is just a thought. But once we write it down, we begin to program the mind to look for opportunities to achieve it. Here are the most effective ways to write the goals to open the subconscious mind.

1.   Must be personal
2.   Must be written in the present tense
3.   Must be specific
4.   Must be positive
5.   Must be empowering
6.   Must include a deadline

Here is an example of how a typical goal might be written:

Increase team sales.

The way that this goal is written, it fails to connect. It does not include the personal, present tense, positive, empowering, specific or the deadline elements of proper goal writing. Remember it's more than just putting it on paper; it's about properly programming your mind. Look at how much more powerful this goal becomes when all six elements are included.

"I lead my team with integrity and develop each member, and that increases our sales 1 million dollars by July 15."

I lead my team (personal/present tense) *with integrity and develop each member,* (positive/empowering) *and that increases our sales 1million dollars* (specific) *by July 15.* (deadline)

Stage Four
- **Action Plan**

If you only did the first three stages, you would be more successful than most in reaching your goals. Largely because of the incredible power that the subconscious mind has when programmed properly. Stage Four, the Action Plan, gives us the steps that we develop to reach our goals. It is the roadmap that we will use. It's important to understand that even the best plans will have to be revised as you go. It is impossible to know everything that you will encounter on the way to reaching the goal. The important thing is that you will be engaged every step of the way. In my opinion one of the most vital parts of the process is knowing the first steps to take and then taking them. The Action Plan is designed to give you those first steps and generate lasting momentum for the duration of the goal reaching process.

The larger the goal, the more detailed the action plan needs to be. There are some goals that may not require an extensive action plan, but all goals need to be accompanied by an action plan regardless of the size.

A typical action plan will:

1.   Break the goal down into smaller goals.
2.   Details the steps necessary to reach the goal.
3.   List the resources needed: human, financial, personal, physical/structural, material ect.
4.   Include an element to measure progress.
5.   Provide a detailed time line.

Stage Five
- **Daily Reaching**

Daily reaching is intended to keep the goal real and alive. So often we get busy with other things and let life sidetrack our plans. The action plan may call for periods where progress is slow and unexciting. The key is to not lose sight of our goal and keep programming our minds to look for the opportunities. Daily reaching is designed to keep us motivated and feeling the emotions of how life will be when we reach the goal.

1.   Write the goal at least once in the morning and once throughout the day ideally close to bedtime. Write the goal in the format as described in stage three. The more you write the goal, the deeper the impression you make on your subconscious. You should always physically write the goal; do not use a computer to type it. It becomes more personal and powerful when it is actually written on a sheet of paper.

2.   Spend at least one minute three times a day visualizing the way you will feel when you reach the goal.

The more time you spend in positive thought about the goals, the more powerful the desire for those goals will become. As the desire increases, so will your action. The goal-reaching program is about action. Take the step, commit and start your goal reaching program today.

Tip #27

Know your stats.

There are two things about a career in sales that all must understand.

1.   You are always self employed. Even if you technically "work" for someone else; you are self employed.

2.   You are the President and Founder of the YOU Corporation. This means that it is your responsibility to make it profitable for your share holders. Your shareholders are yourself and your family.

With those two points established you must know some basic information about your newly discovered You Corporation.

Here are some basic stats that you should know…

- How many marketing touches it takes to secure an appointment?

- How many marketing touches it takes to generate a new client?

- What is your conversion rate?

- What percentage of your business is new vs. repeat?

- What percentage of your business are referrals?

- What is your most profitable marketing effort?

- What percentage of your business gets returned?

- What is your average sale amount?

If you don't know the answers to these questions you need to find them out. Without this information you are losing a powerful tool to analyze your business. A lot of sales people fail to run their career like a business. They take a very casual approach to their career and the result is never achieving the success they are capable of. They allow their careers to be managed by others and never take control.

The professional understands that:

(A)   They are running a business, often times within a business.

(B)   In order to maximize that business they must be able to accurately analyze their business.

(C)   By knowing their stats they can improve on areas that are lacking and increase the areas they are having success in.

A career in sales is a career in business. Begin to run your career that way and you will soon discover streams of income you were overlooking.

Tip #28

Create a professional presentation.

A professional presentation is a must. There are no short cuts when it comes to presenting. The presentation is the crucial point to either opening the deal in a timely manner or losing the sale altogether. Each industry will have different presentation needs; however a well thought-out and scripted presentation that flows like a casual conversation is ideal.

Many sales people have the ability to think "quick on their feet" and become lazy. They achieve moderate success and believe that there is no need to properly prepare. The sales professional is always looking to seize opportunities. One way they do this is with a presentation that is well worded and delivered with precision. Regardless if you sell TV's or jet airplanes you must create a professional presentation.

Tip #29

Know what your client looks like.

Not physically, but what their needs, wants, or desires are. You want to be able to recognize them immediately. In addition you need to be able to describe them to others when you are networking. This allows you to capitalize on your networking efforts. Seek to make it easy for others to assist you.

Valuable resources are wasted by not knowing what your client looks like. If I know my ideal client is a technology business with 15 employees or less why would I invest in marketing to a larger company that operates in the restaurant industry? Yet many sales people do just that. Know what your client looks like and market to that target group.

Tip #30

Smile!

You will make more sells with a smile than a frown.

Tip #31

Be interesting.

Most people would rather do business with people they find interesting than people who they do not. Think about what makes you unique and interesting to others and work to bring those qualities out during your interactions.

Tip #32

Understand the power of words.

Well constructed word can create powerful feelings and thoughts. As you create your sales presentation construct your points paying close attention to the wording you use. Think of the emotion you are trying to create and work from there as a baseline.

Tip #33

Sell with stories.

Stories connect faster and stronger than facts and figures. Mixing a story with facts will appeal to most personalities. When selling with stories make sure the story brings value to the process. Becoming a good story teller will help you create a relationship with your clients and will serve to make you interesting. If you don't have stories that are relevant then do some research and find stories that are relevant and include them into the selling process.

Tip #34

Create unique replies.

Everyday regardless of who you are or what you sell people will ask you this very simple question. How are you today? The most common response is "I'm ok I guess." STOP!!! Who wants to be around someone like that? This is a negative response to a neutral question. Your ok? You guess? Don't be ok and don't guess. Be something more than ok. Be something positive and declare it don't guess it.

I developed a response based upon the day of the week. You will be shocked at the smiles and response you will get back using this technique.

Question: How are you today?

The response:

Monday: *I'm Marvelous*

Tuesday: *I'm Terrific*

Wednesday: *I'm Wonderful*

Thursday: *I'm Thrilled*

Friday: *I'm Fantastic*

Saturday: *I'm Super*

Sunday: *I'm Sensational*

You should begin to create these types of positive replies with all the common questions that you encounter on a daily basis. Every time you give a positive response you feed your mind positive information and over time this can help produce positive feelings and emotions.

A good example of a unique reply is in action at Chick-fil-A they always end with "It's my pleasure to serve you." That's unique; it's noticeable and leaves a positive impression. Give people something new and refreshing. They will take notice and you will have begun breaking down the walls of preprogrammed responses. This encourages others to give you a real response as well. If nothing else you will stand out from the other people they encountered that day.

Tip #35

Integrity.

It is a must for the sales professional. Integrity means doing the right thing regardless of the outcome. It is having a solid foundation of morals and ethics and being uncorrupted and honest. In the profession of sales, integrity is the single most important quality. It trumps all others. It is far more crucial than having the best product. It is more important than having a great presentation. What good is a great presentation if the person delivering it cannot be trusted? Integrity is everything. Make sure that yours isn't for sale! Here is a Chinese proverb to remember:

To starve to death is a small thing to lose ones integrity is a large thing.

This is especially true in sales, if you have no integrity you will certainly starve to death.

Tip #36

Personalize the experience.

Thank you notes that are hand written still remain a cost effective tool. Take the time to write a note, most of your competitors won't.

Tip #37

Always ask for referrals.

Referrals are the life blood of your sales career. They give you immediate access and generally will allow you to open the deal much faster. You should never ask for a referral until you have been successful in exceeding their needs. Too often referrals are asked for at the point that the sale is made, before the product or service has ever been delivered. If you ask before they know that you are worth the referral, they will be very hesitant and will hold back their quality referrals. Those are the ones you want! Take the extra time to show your client that they are your most important priority not your next sell.

Tip #38

Ask open ended questions.

When creating your presentation make sure that you engage your future client with open ended questions designed to create a specific and predictable response. An open ended question is a question that can't be answered with just a yes or no. Open ended questions help you to engage your client and will also allow you to gain valuable insight into their needs, wants, desires and problems.

Tip #39

View objections as opportunities.

Objections are always part of the sales process much like getting wet is part of swimming. Understand that an objection is an opportunity to understand where your client is in the sales process. It also allows you to properly reposition the product to move deeper into the process. Don't run away from them. Don't hide from them and most importantly don't fear them. Embrace them as the opportunity that they are.

Tip #40

The gate keeper is not evil.

They are doing a job and if you approach them with a negative view you are already forecasting a negative experience. Choose to view them as information ambassadors. Treat them with over the top courtesy and they generally respond the same.

Tip #41

Remember names.

One of the top tips for your personal and business life is to remember people's names. In his book *How to Win Friends and Influence People*, Dale Carnegie says "Remember that a person's name is the sweetest and most important sound in any language." I believe that this statement has even more truth for us today than years ago. Society as a whole does not put an emphasis on this very simple skill. I call it a skill because it is just that, a skill. You will either choose to invest in developing it or not. When you choose to make the extra effort to remember names and connect with people it makes a positive impact.

One of the best examples I have witnessed of this was by Lee Goble. At the time I met Lee; he was a State Sales Manager for a Fortune 500 company and had a sales team of over 400 people. It was remarkable to watch Lee connect with his team. He not only knew his team members names but their spouse and often times their children's names. It amazed me the effort he made to remember names and details about each one of them. As a result Lee built an incredible team that won many awards. People enjoy feeling important and remembering their name is a good place to start.

Tip #42

Stop Talking!

Often times as sales people we have a tendency to believe we are not selling if we are not talking. I have found just the opposite to be the case. If most sales people would stop talking and start listening they would open more sales, make more money, help more people, and have more business than they could handle. Stop talking!

Tip #43

Know the P + S = O
Sales Formula.

This is a formula that I developed years ago to keep focused and uncover the information necessary to open the deal. I have developed countless professionals using this very formula. It is simple, versatile, and very powerful. I use this formula in every aspect of my personal business from marketing, presentations, new business development, and, of course, to help develop professionals.

Problems + Solutions = Opportunity

Problems:

This encompasses wants, needs and desires.

Solutions:

These are the ways you can solve or satisfy the problem, wants, needs, and desires.

Opportunity:

Anything that can create a positive result.

When creating your presentation, developing a new business, or selling your product/service you must find the problem, have the solution, and an opportunity will be created.

Understand that this formula applies to all parts of your life. From leadership to relationships and everything in between:

Problems + Solutions = Opportunities.

Tip #44

Your time is valuable.

If you don't value your time then chances are; no one else will either. If you have clients that are always late and disorganized for meetings; they don't value your time. Your clients must value your time as an expert in your market. Don't work with future clients, current clients or other sales staff that waste your time.

There are so many distractions that can pull you away from income producing activities that you must take an active approach to investing your time wisely. It is imperative in a sales career that you value your time and demand that others do as well.

Tip #45

Use a time management system.

Most sales people waste more time thinking about what they are going to do than actually doing it. I have found that the most successful sales people are the ones that use a time management system to keep them focused and on track.

Time is the one thing that just doesn't care about who you are or where you've been. Time doesn't discriminate between the rich or poor, young or old. There are twenty-four hours in a day and sixty minutes in an hour. We all have the same access to time; therefore we have the same opportunity to leverage it. What separates successful sales people from others is what they do with their time: how they manage it and more importantly how they invest it. Time is a valuable resource, and without it nothing else seems to matter. The key is to leverage time, so you can maximize the harvest from it. The first step of being able to leverage time is to value it. Secondly we must invest the majority of our time in activities that produce high-end results.

The program that I currently use and teach is a combination from a number of systems that I have learned through the years. I have found if the system itself is time consuming, then it defeats the point. I purposely streamlined this program and kept it as simple as possible. The most important thing to know is whatever system you use will be more effective than not using any system at all.

I break my tasks into four categories.

1. **Have to Do**
    - These are tasks that produce high-end results.
    - They have serious repercussions if not completed.
    - These activities have firm deadlines.

2. **Need to Do**
    - These are tasks that you need to accomplish.
    - They have a moderate end result.
    - They have some repercussions if not completed.
    - They should have deadlines.

3. **Might Do**
    - These are tasks that you would accomplish if time permits.
    - They have low-end results.
    - They have no repercussions if not completed.
    - They wouldn't have deadlines.

4. **Could Delegate**
   - These are tasks that you could delegate to another.
   - They could vary from high, medium, and low-end results.
   - They could carry repercussions if not completed.
   - If delegated, they will always have a deadline.

Under each category you will prioritize each task/project by three elements.

Deadline:
When does it need to be completed?

Degree of Return:
Is this a high return of low return project/task?

Importance:
Are other team members waiting for this to complete their work?

Assigning a letter A-Z to that task/project under one of the four categories, begin with A and finish that task/project before moving onto B. Never work on a *Need to Do* task/project if you have something in the *Have to Do* category. Eliminate all unnecessary bouncing back and forth from task to task while completing only a portion at a time. The practice of task hopping generally steals time from you. The point is to invest the majority of time in the activities that produce high-end results. The balancing act is not to invest more time than necessary with each project. As stated there are many systems available for you to use. Find the one that works for you and use it!

Tip #46

Destination work? WRONG!

Work is an activity not a destination. Just because you are physically at the place that you call "work" doesn't mean that you are working. Often times we fool ourselves into thinking as long as we are occupying space in a building then we are working. Make it a point to do the activity of work and not confuse it with the destination.

Tip #47

Know the four personalities types.

Understanding your client's personality type is a key strategy in being able to interact with them in a way that encourages them to buy. It is guaranteed to increase your sales by having fundamental knowledge on this subject.

The system outlined here is the system that I teach in my sales, leadership and personal success development workshops. This system is easy to remember and fast to apply.

The system uses two categories Expressiveness and Forcefulness. Within each of the categories there are two classifications; they are Less and More.

Less or More Forceful:

The word forceful in this application has nothing to do with the physical application of strength and everything to do with the words, demeanor, and the directness in which the person speaks and acts.

Less or More Expressive:

The word expressive in this application refers to how personable and friendly they are, if they are easy going, open to communication, and inviting.

When put on a chart it looks like this:

Less Expressive

Less Forceful

More Forceful

More Expressive

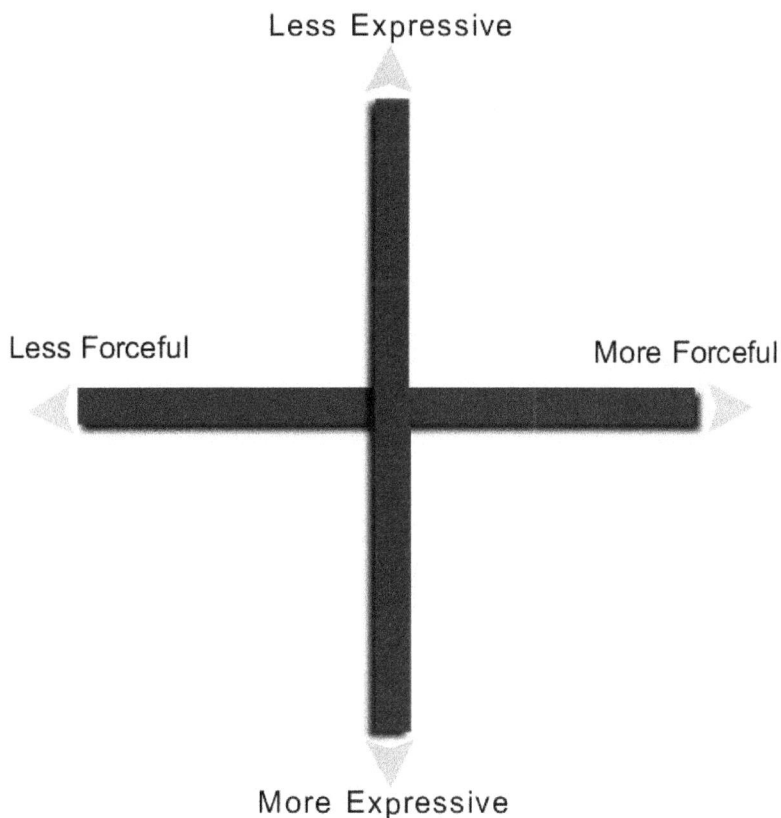

The system uses four distinct personality types. I use descriptive words for those personality types; they are listed in bold with the common clinical term in parenthesis. I encourage you to use whatever term you find easier to remember and associate with the character traits. The most important part is being able to immediately classify the person you are interacting with. This allows you to adjust your sales presentation to the style that best suits their personality.

C.P.A. (Analytical)

The C.P.A. is a well-organized individual. This person operates in a very structured environment. They love facts and figures, and enjoy researching every possible angle. They work well in a task-orientated culture. These individuals tend to make slower decisions and base those decisions on facts and data not personal feelings. They thrive in environments where they can use their intellect; they are deliberate and logical. Often times these individuals like to have authority. The C.P.A. avoids confrontation.

General (Driver)
The General is the person who is on the move; they get things done and tend to be very goal driven. They have little time for people who waste time and don't pull their own weight. These individuals carry themselves in a very rigid and upright manner; they walk fast and always seem to be in a hurry. They thrive in high-pressure situations. At times they come off as offensive because of their lack of small talk. Their interests are focused on results not people. Generals make quick and swift decisions based on a fast assessment of the facts. They are decisive and assertive and would be considered risk takers. Generals love authority and do not mind confrontation.

Oprah (Amiable)

The Oprah is a person who needs to connect to other people. They are into feelings and emotions and invest heavily in personal relationships. They like to share and expect others to share with them. These individuals base their decisions on personal feelings and the ability to judge the people involved in the situation or presenting the idea. They are loyal and perceptive, and they have the ability to make decisions quickly depending on the circumstances. They tend to try to resolve any situation with all parties feeling like they have gained. They avoid confrontation.

Entertainer (Expressive)

Entertainers are always on stage. They tend to be the life of the party; they love attention and are sociable. They are "into" what others think about them and tend to invest in appearances. They base decisions on what other respected individuals think. Routines and structure are not important to them. They are more focused on people than tasks, and are enthusiastic and dramatic. Generally they possess shorter attention spans and will postpone making decisions. Entertainers love authority but avoid confrontation.

Putting the four personality types on the chart gives a visual reference.

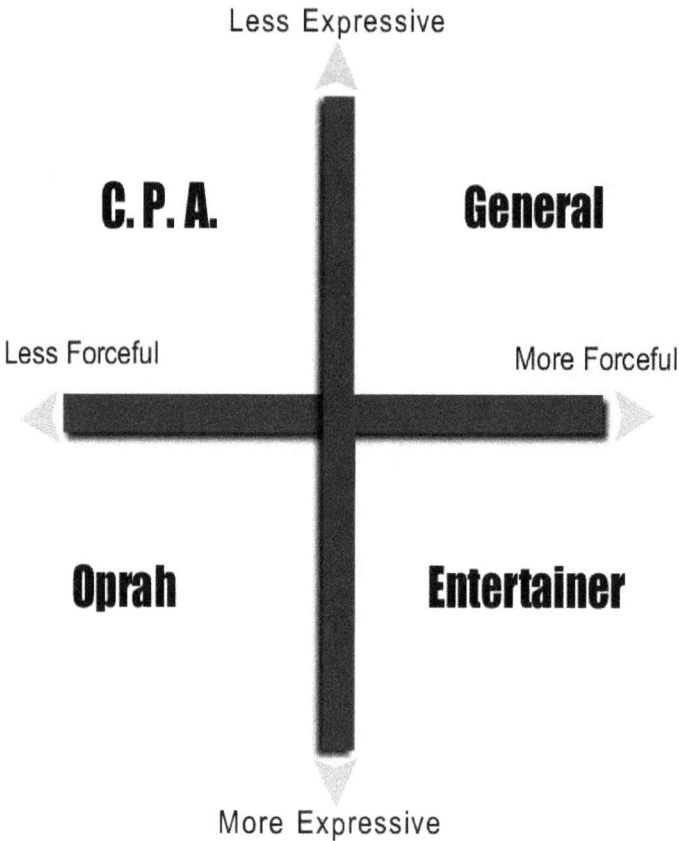

Less Expressive

C. P. A.   **General**

Less Forceful   More Forceful

Oprah   **Entertainer**

More Expressive

Knowing that the C.P.A. is well organized and likes facts and figures, how will you approach the sale when working with a C.P.A.? You will need to have printed, organized facts, figures and stats, available for them to analyze. Generally they will want to look at these facts in writing it will not be enough for you to just quote them. However you should be able to reference this type of information quickly without hesitation. They are well organized so they expect that of you as well. C.P.A.'s make decisions only after analyzing and researching the information. If you press to much you will find that they will shut down. Their work space is neat and orderly and everything has its place.

If working with the General then you will need to speed up, cut to the chase, and get to the point. Don't waste time with needless chatter. Identify the goals that they need help reaching and with confidence, clearly describe how your product/service will benefit them. A typical General's office will have plaques and awards that show others how important they are.

When you are working with an Oprah you need to build the relationship and connect with them on a personal level. They will typically have pictures of people and places that they love surrounding them and are willing to share details about each one. There is danger in moving too fast with an Oprah they need to feel that you care about them and what they are doing. You must connect first before a sale will be made.

If you don't know the dynamics of the Entertainers then you will most likely waste valuable time. The real key with Entertainers is getting a firm commitment and getting them to take action. Many sales people will be drawn in by the excitement and the over the top personalities and fail to take the steps to move the relationship further into the sales process. They discover that they have lost the initial momentum and are unable to get the Entertainer to recommit or even take a follow up appointment.

Entertainers are great for referral business, because of their personalities they tend to network with a lot of people. When you exceed their expectations they will tell others about it. This is always great for your business.

By now you should be matching people in your life with these four personality styles. You might be thinking that they tend to be a combination of a few, which is absolutely correct. At different times and in different situations, you will see a shift in the personality type, however we all have a default personality type that is more dominate. The ability to recognize quickly what type of personality you are working with and modify your approach to fit that person's personality will make it more comfortable for them to move the relationship further into the sales process. In situations that you are presenting to more than one personality type attempt to identify the person who has the most authority and influence to make the decision and work your presentation 60-70% to that style. If one cannot be identified then you should use a presentation that includes elements for all four personality styles.

Tip #48

Develop your marketing system.

Regardless if you represent a national company who invests millions of dollars each year in marketing campaigns or you are a sole proprietor that has a limited marketing budget; you need to develop your own marketing system. We know from Tip #18 that marketing is anything that you do that positively promotes you or your business. This obviously encompasses a wide variety of activities. The system needs to be effective and efficient but doesn't need to be overcomplicated. However, it must contain measurable elements. The system that I use and teach contains these key elements.

Lead Creation:

These are the activities you perform to create leads. Ideally you should be able to measure the effectiveness of each activity and calculate your return on investment. In most cases you will have multiple lead creation sources.

Sales Cycle:

There are two tracks within the sales cycle. Either the *Yes Track* or the *Not Now Track*. <u>There is not a no track!</u>

Yes Track:

In this track you are working with your client to open the deal. You build the relationship as you walk them through each step of the sales cycle. For some industries this can be very extensive and for others this is a quick process. Regardless you should know each step to ensure this is a smooth process.

Not Now Track:

This is exactly what it says. When you're marketing efforts are targeted, intelligent and systematical, you will be marketing to people or organizations are your ideal clients. When you have a quality product/service combined with targeted marketing it is only a matter of time before they become your client. This is one of the reasons I use the word "future client" as opposed to perspective client.

Client Retention/Farming Program:

This is the area where you exceed the client's expectations and continue to provide excellent client service. After they become your client then they transition into your farming program. You continue to cultivate a positive relationship and prepare for ongoing sales as well as referrals. Each industry will farm clients slightly different. Some common techniques are newsletters, birthday cards, holiday cards, special discounts, exclusive memberships, client appreciation days, t-shirts, free services, the possibilities are only limited to your creativity. Anything that you can throughout the year that gives value and benefit to your client is acceptable. Of course nothing trumps excellent client service.

Warming Cycle:

This is the most neglected category by most sales people. If the typical sales person in your industry opens 1 out of 10 appointments/presentations, what do they do with the other 9 they were not able to open immediately? They forget about them! This drives up the cost of your lead creation and you miss the opportunity of being able to open the deal at a later time. Will there ever be a month that you will not want business? Exactly; so warm up these future clients in your warming cycle. Not only will some of these move out of the warming cycle back into the sales cycle, you will be surprised at how it will create new leads for you as well. Remember, the goal is to create access and influence (Tip #22) and that is what the Warming Cycle is designed to do. Some of the activities you do as part of your Client Retention/Farming Program will be able to be used in the Warming Cycle as well.

Client Retention
Farming Program

Lead Creation

New Client

**Move Through
Each Phase of the
Sales Cycle**

Sales Cycle

Warming Cycle

Yes
Track

Not Now
Track

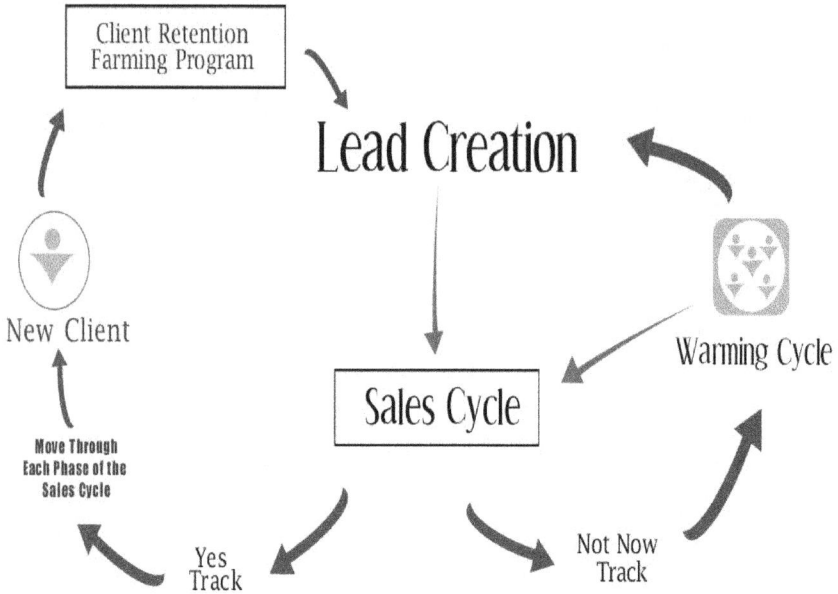

The sales professional uses a marketing system to ensure they are maximizing all resources and are creating a constant flow of new clients and business. Many of these components can be automated so you are able to leverage technology (Tip# 99). The system is flexible to the degree that you determine the kind of activities and the costs for the Warming Cycle, Farming Program, and Lead Creation. The activities will vary from industry to industry and even from product to product however the basic system remains the same. Once you know the system you can replicate it over and over again applying it to any product or service to produce a steady and predictable stream of results.

Tip #49

Use language that sets you apart.

Unfortunately the majority of sales people will be trained and not developed. They will be drilled to say the same things as the rest of the sales team and they will be taught the standard vanilla language that is passed from industry to industry. With each pass the compliance department strips it down even further. At the end you have small sound bites glued together and approved for sales people that will be trained and programmed like robots. This cycle is counterproductive for everyone involved.

Seek to use language that triggers emotion and a positive response. Stay away from the standard sales language everyone else is using.

Here are a few examples.

Standard Way: *"I specialize in working with small business owners."*

New Way: *"My passion is helping business owners just like you in the Denver (name the city, county or part of the country you serve) area."*

In the standard way we are using the old "specialize" word many sales people love to use. Thinking it makes them sound important. However where is the focus; on the client or themselves? On themselves, what does specialize really mean to your client? When we use the words passion, helping, and just like you, it triggers a different level of emotion that the word specialize is not able to do. Just because you specialize doesn't mean you enjoy it. Nor does it mean you chose to specialize in that particular area. It is very possible your job description requires you to specialize in it. However, if it's your passion to help people in a   particular situation or with a particular problem it creates the impression you care and have a genuine interest.

Standard Way: *"When you buy this TV you will see the quality."*

New Way: *"By owning this TV you will experience the quality every time you turn it on."*

In the standard way the first comparison is with the words *buy vs. owning*. The word buy hits the subconscious mind as spending money while owning conveys pride, prestige, and in many cases even a sense of power. The second comparison is with the phrases you will see the *quality vs. you will experience the quality*. Which language paints a more vivid and powerful emotion?

Avoid the canned vanilla language and construct emotion producing language that helps you connect to your perspective client and move the relationship further into the sales process.

Tip #50

Exceed after sales expectations.

This will explode your business. Most sales people will do a fair job leading up to the sale but once the purchase has been made they move quickly to the next client and forget about the one they just opened. As sales professional you realize some of your client's biggest concerns are not having after the sale service. If you do this one thing great, you will have a strong repeat client base that will be an active marketing machine (Tip 66) for you.

Tip #51

Create a unique Tweet Speech.

Years ago this was called an elevator speech. The idea was to "pitch" or sale yourself to the person in the time it took to ride an elevator. Times have changed and so has the approach. The elevator speech is too long and the "pitch" is extinct (even though some refuse to accept it). People today have less time to give you and will immediately tune out a sales pitch.

The new generation sales professional must understand the focus is always on the clients and establishing trust. An unsolicited mini commercial is not the way to do that. Here are some guidelines to follow when creating your Tweet Speech.

Brief: Keep it short, 140 characters or less.

Personal: I or we, instead of the company I work for.

Interesting: Boring doesn't work.

Benefit: Needs to be obvious but not stated.

Target Market Specific: By stating the subject you are separating those who could use your product or service from those who have no interest in it.

Unique: Pick up lines don't work for single guys or sales people.

Honest: Don't insult people with phony lines.

Many times people will ask you the "what do you do" question even though they have absolutely zero interest in what you do. They are asking the question because it is safe and they don't know what else to say. This is an opportunity for you to market your message so it sparks enough curiosity that they ask the follow up question. When they ask the follow up question, you have created *access* as discussed in Tip #22. Understand your access might be limited so you need to maximize the opportunity by being prepared. The sales professional takes the time to script out a response that allows them to capitalize on the opportunity.

Below is an example a life insurance agent might use. It encompasses the seven guidelines.

Question : What do you do?

TWEET SPEECH: *"I help families solve some of life's most difficult financial problems today, so they don't become reality tomorrow."*

Follow up Question: How do you do that?

Once they ask the follow up question you must move into a casual conversation asking questions that help uncover a want, need, desire or problem that your product or service can solve.

Tip #52

Dress the part for your market.

How do the people who advise your clients dress. That is how you should dress. There is an urge to always dress casual. Refuse the urge and dress the part of a successful, confident adviser.

Tip #53

Iron your shirt and shine your shoes.

Nothing screams unprofessional more than un-shined shoes and a wrinkled shirt/blouse. Your appearance is a reflection of your work! Iron your shirt/blouse and shine your shoes; you'll feel better about yourself and look better too.

Tip #54

Watch how much you drink at conferences and meetings.

Most of the time there will be an open bar at sales conferences. It is a bad idea for you to overindulge. While at the time the other sales staff may find it amusing, you don't want to get the reputation of being the one that can't control their drinking. Remember your sales managers and upper management are at those meetings and a bad experience with you can have negative effects on your career.

Tip #55

Avoid the Harvard Syndrome.

Often sales people like to dazzle clients with their knowledge of a product or industry. They use complex language that leaves their clients confused. There is real danger in doing this. Not only do you run the risk of not making the sell, you open yourself up for confusion as to the expectations of your product or service. Don't over talk to the client but don't under talk to the client either. Speak at the level that your client will understand. The point is to open the deal. You increase the chance of doing that if they understand what you are saying.

Tip #56

Limit your slides.

If you use a slide show as part of your presentation be aware that less is more. The average sales person uses slides *as* their presentation. They painfully read the slides to their audience while the audience drifts off to another land called boredom. If a slide show could "open the deal" your company would not be paying you. Slide shows are used to enhance your presentation not make the presentation; you must still be engaging. Be careful of information overload and remember that less is more when it comes to slides.

Tip #57

Provide over the top client service.

In most markets today virtually no client service exists. You should strive to provide world class client service. This is a sure way to stand out. If you are ever going to successfully build a referral based career this will be an important factor.

Tip #58

Assume the sale.

If you represent a quality product/service that solves your client's problems, needs, wants or desires then why won't they want to own it? Enter into the meeting with the confidence that you and your product/service are superior and it is just a matter of time and everyone will own it. With that new found confidence, why would you ever do anything other than assume the sale.

Tip #59

Ask for the sale.

Many sales people spend an hour explaining the benefits of their product/service and then never ask for the sale. This is puzzling. Everyone involved knows you are there representing a product/service that is for sale. It shouldn't offend them or catch them off guard when you expect them to purchase your product. So why do so many sales people fail to ask for the sale? The first step of the process is entering into the meeting assuming the sale; with this mentality it is only natural to make the next step of asking/confirming the sale. If you struggle with this element of your sales career spend some time developing a phrase you feel comfortable saying that asks/confirms the sale. If you will do this you will see your sales make a quantum leap forward!

Tip #60

Find a phrase.

Finding a phrase that you can use to determine where your client is in the buying process is crucial. Take for example the phrase listed below.

If I can_____*(explain the benefit of your service/product)* for _____ *(describe the terms)* can I count on your business?

By using this phrase the perspective client will have to reply with one of three options.

1.   Yes, you can count on my business

2.   No

3.   I'm not sure

If they chose option one; complete your sales process immediately. If they chose option two or three your reply will be "What will it take for me to be able to?" Again this is putting it on them to tell you what the real issue is.

Using the words "can I count on your business" has a powerful psychological effect. In essence they have just given you their word that you can count on them. If they go back on their word they have broken a promise to you. This makes most people feel like they are a person that cannot be counted on. No one likes to think of themselves as that. So using this phrase, or one similar, implies a social contract and in the subconscious they are entering into an obligation with you.

A few alternatives to the "count on your business" are...

Is there any reason why you wouldn't do business with me?

When would you like us to set up delivery?

When do you want us to begin?

Is there anything that would prevent us from doing business together?

There are endless possibilities. The point is you need to create a phrase that you are comfortable delivering that causes them to commit to the sale or tell you what else they need for you to do for them to commit to the sale.

Tip #61

The three powerful "F" words.

Perhaps the most effective tool to engage a concern that your client is contained in the three powerful "F" words. They are, Feel, Felt, Found. This concept has been taught for years by all the leading experts and still remains the most under used tool in the sales person's tool box. The key is to identify the area of concern your client has raised and then use the feel, felt, found to reassure the client and move forward with the sales process. Let's examine each word closer.

Feel:

This is how you are acknowledging their concern. The word feel is letting them know that you understand.

Felt:

Here is where you let them know that their feelings are normal, that they have the right to have these concerns and feelings.

Found:

This is the area where you are conveying to them that you are the expert and you have led others just like them through this process and that you are going to do the same for them. The best practice is to use a high profile client, someone in their industry that they would recognize to link them together. It serves to let them know you have worked with that particular client (thus building confidence in you and your ability) and also pays them a compliment by classifying them in the same category with the high profile client. It subtly says to the client that if others are moving forward with this product or service then they should as well.

Here is an example of how it works.

Mrs. Jones I understand how you *feel*. Mr. Smith at Inspire Consultants, *felt* the same way as you do now when I/we initially discussed a plan similar to this with him. However what he and I both *found* was that......

This is a simple formula that is time tested and proven. I have seen firsthand the impact of these four words can have on sales careers. I encourage you to work with these "F' words and make them part of your sales response.

I can understand if you feel a little nervous about using this "F" word strategy. From personal experience when I first started to use the formula I felt I little nervous myself, but what I found is that by acknowledging and then relating to my clients concerns both my comfort level and theirs increased. As a result my sales career exploded.

Tip #62

Leverage Permission Phrases.

Permission phrases are the most unknown sales techniques in my opinion. Permission phrases build rapport, show respect, and allow you in many cases to disarm the perspective client so that they will speak more open with you. In essence you are both agreeing to cut out the charades that sometimes bog down the sales process.

Here are five permission phrases that you can begin to use immediately.

- *May I speak frank/straight with you?*
- *With your permission I would like to....*
- *If I could...*
- *Will you allow me to...*
- *If it's alright with you let me cut all the fluff and give you the facts that you'll want to know to be able to make a decision.*

WARNING:

Never use the word honest in a permission phrase. This leaves the impression that you have been less than honest up to that point and you normally are not honest. Let me make this very clear that you only use the permission phrase from a position of confidence and authority not of weakness. If you struggle with projecting confidence then this technique will not be effective for you.

Tip #63

Counter "I need some time to think about it."

Most sales people stop right there with their presentation. This is by far one of the most effective push offs used by people. We know your chances of opening the deal decreases every minute when they give you this push off. So you must attempt to reengage and get the deal opened. Obviously different markets have a different sales cycle and you will need to establish what the cycle is for the industry and you personally. If you have reached the point that this push off is a deal killer then you need to question their statement.

<u>Perspective Client-</u> *I need some time.....*

<u>Sales Professional-</u> *May I speak frank/straight with you?* (Permission Phrase)

Perspective Client- *Sure/Yes*

Sales Professional- *Based on my experience when I hear that, it means a few things. Either I didn't do a good job explaining the value/benefits of my service and your unsure, or you have no interest in my service and you don't want to hurt my feelings.* (Pause, slight laugh) *So which one is it?* (Stay quiet and let them speak)

If you want to increase your sales you must be able to counter the "time" push off. Remember that you are attempting to uncover the real reason why they are not moving forward. Rarely is it that they just need time to think about it.

Tip #64

Plan your day the night before.

The average sales person does not preplan their next day's activities. However for the sales professional a key strategy to increasing production is preplanning so that time is maximized. Without a preplan most of us get drawn into activities that are not income producing. Professionals know being pulled in a direction that does not advance a sale is in essence costing them money.

Tip #65

Protect YOUR name brand.

Everyone has a name and so everyone has a name brand. However, few sales people understand the importance of it. They represent any company that promises a higher commission regardless of the quality of the product or service. They ruin their name brand and in doing so ruin the market for themselves. One must be diligent in choosing only the best companies and products to represent.

In the course of a sales career you will be presented with many opportunities. Some of those opportunities may come in the way of representing different products/services within the same organization or with a different organization. As we discussed in Tip #22 the first step of any sales process is having access and influence. The natural place that it exists is in your established client base. Having the availability to market to your established client base is a huge asset. That can only occur if you have provided quality products and exceptional client service in the past.

Think about what you want your clients to associate your name with? What do you want your name brand known for? Your actions, words, behaviors and products/services must all be consistent with that thing. Companies come and go, products fade away, but you will carry your name brand with you for life. Protect it and make sure it is not for sale!

*One must always comply with all contractual agreements when marketing to existing clients.

Tip #66

Establish marketing machines.

Marketing machines are partnerships that fall under the lead creation and warming cycle of your marketing plan. A marketing machine helps you spread your message and produces leads for you. Let's focus our attention on the two most common types. Virtual and Actual.

Virtual:

This is a technology based lead creation source. This can be a platform you create or one that is created for you. It can encompass websites, blogs, reviews, industry specific programs or paying to have leads created for you. Typically all of these are being created by technology and there is not a personal touch.

Actual:

There are two forms in the Actual category. They are Organic and Developed.

Organic:

This is where your referrals come into play, they are grown from your relationships and commitment to your clients. You should always be able to obtain referrals from your clients. That is the minimum standard. Ultimately what you want to do is turn your clients into fans. I define a fan as*: Someone who is actively and enthusiastically sharing your product/service or message.* In essence a fan shares you. This is very powerful to your lead creation program. Your goal should always be to turn your clients into fans.

Developed:

There are two classifications in this category. They are casual and structured.

- *Casual:* This can be as simple as a local business exchange club or two people agreeing to refer each other business.

- *Structured:* These are strategic partnerships. These partnerships generally have agreed upon terms and compensation is involved.

A sure way to explode your business is to establish a series of marketing machines so that the streams of future clients flow to you.

Here are five keys to remember when setting up marketing machines.

1.   Establish yourself as an expert.

2.   Only work with credible people or organizations.

3.   Open the deal to make clients. Provide world class service to make fans.

4.   Clearly let them know how they can help you. Describe to them what your ideal client looks like.

5.   Become a marketing machine for them.

There is perhaps no better way to increase your business than partnering with others to help get your message out. By developing these marketing machines you are creating strategic partnerships that allow you to touch more people resulting in increased production.

Tip #67

View yourself as self employed.

I touched briefly on this in Tip # 27, regardless if you are self employed or employed by a company with a monthly draw, you are self employed. The days of working for one company for 40 years are gone. The market today is fast paced and is more global than many care to recognize. When you make the mental shift to viewing yourself as self employed you position yourself to take all the steps necessary as a business owner to make yourself profitable.

To be profitable, business owners must stay on top of their market and search for new technology and tools to be competitive. While most "employees" take a more passive approach to their employability, the professional understands the culture has changed. As a professional you must embrace these changes and continue to evolve. The market moves at such a fast pace that keeping up is really falling behind. This means investing in your continued development through courses designed to keep you competitive. From technology classes to professional coaching you must be responsible for yourself. The old mind set of letting a company keep you "trained" is over. It is crucial to view yourself as a business owner and make your business as competitive and profitable as you can.

Tip #68

Remember it's not personal.

Often times we get discouraged when a sale doesn't happen and take the rejection and make it personal. This is unwise and will lead you down a dark path that has claimed the career of many sales people. It's not personal rejection. In fact it may have absolutely nothing to do with you. In most cases it has everything to do with them. Perhaps they aren't ready for your product or service. It could be there is something in their personal life preventing them from making clear decisions. Regardless don't take it personal. I have a rule that I will never take it more personal then they make it. Unless someone says directly to me "I'm not purchasing this product because I don't like you." I choose to believe the issue must be with them and not with me.

With that being said, self evaluation is always necessary to determine how we can perform better and help our clients come to the purchasing decision. Self evaluation to improve and personal rejection is two very different things. One is positive the other is not. Just for a moment think about your favorite store. If you go there and look but don't purchase something they don't close the doors and go home and have a terrible day. They keep the doors open and continue to sell to the next person. So should you. Avoid getting sucked into the personal rejection black hole. Keep selling.

Tip #69

ATTITUDE!

I believe that attitude is everything. How you approach a situation will largely determine the outcome of that situation. Years ago I was introduced to a way to illustrate the important role attitude plays in our life. If you were to take each letter of the word attitude and place the number for the position it occupies in the alphabet with it, it would look like this.

A=1, **T**=20, **T**=20, **I**=9, **T**=20, **U**=21, **D**=4, **E**=5 $= 100$

When you add those numbers up you get 100. The point is your attitude matters one hundred percent of the time. I like to take it a step further and say not only does it matter one hundred percent of the time but that you are in control of it one hundred percent of the time.

So often we give the power to control our attitude to other people. Perhaps it's something someone says or does that ruins our attitude and in turn ruins our day. This is foolish. No one can control your attitude unless you allow them to. Make the choice to have a positive attitude and be in control of it 100% of the time.

Tip #70

Avoid the water cooler.

The water cooler is a symbol of any place that others congregate. This area will suck time away from a sales person quick. This is typically where those who are under performing hangout to make excuses for their lack luster performance. The professionals are not where the other sales people are they are where the clients are and that is not your water cooler. Get out to where your future clients are and sell. Those hanging around the cooler are broke, if you hang out there long enough you will be too.

Tip #71

Be on time.

Being late to an appointment is a sign of disrespect and it says to the other person you do not value their time. Let them know you put a high value on their time and yours. Be prepared, be professional and be on time!

Tip #72

Keep a calendar.

I'm always shocked at how many sales people do not keep a calendar for appointments. There are at least two reasons for keeping a good accurate calendar. The fist one is obvious, so you don't miss appointments. The second one however is less obvious; it is to give the appearance that you are busy conducting other business daily. Who would you feel more confident in, someone who is busy and in demand or someone who seems to have a lot of free time on their hands? Exactly. Get a calendar!

Tip #73

Take notes.

During the sales process it is imperative you take notes on important topics discussed. This allows you to keep a file you can go back to for future reference. It also gives the appearance you are engaged and alert by taking notes. Be aware there is a fine line between taking notes and being involved in the discussion, or taking notes and being involved in taking notes. Take the necessary notes but most importantly be engaged in the discussion.

Tip #74

Use a yellow tablet.

Never use a white spiral tablet for taking notes. I recommended using a yellow tablet that is bound at the top. School children and order takers use white spiral notebooks, not professionals. Keep in mind you are a professional in all aspects of your selling career and it is important you pay attention to the small details.

Tip #75

Return emails and phone calls promptly.

You should be returning phone calls and emails as quickly as possible, but never later than 12 hours. If you're going to be out of the office have an auto responder set up to notify your clients so they will know when to expect the follow up. This simple rule alone will help you stand out above your competition.

Tip #76

Never discount people.

You should always make an attempt to recognize and connect with the people around you. Often sales people are focused on the decision makers and fail to understand how they treat or connect with the supporting figures can potentially play a large role in the final outcome. Practice connecting; take a general interest in all people regardless of their position within the company. Never discount people and always treat them with respect.

Tip #77

Testimonials are powerful.

Testimonials can come in various forms and can be used in a number of media and or copy applications. Always search your clients for testimonials so that you have a resource to pull from when needed. The sales professional understands how to leverage testimonials and knows they help pave the way to a deeper sales relationship. Let's look at the power of the testimonial from four perspectives.

Person Giving the Testimonial:

When properly positioned it produces a feeling of importance and respect. The fact you and others value their opinion creates a positive view of the relationship.

Person Receiving the Testimonial:

It provides reassurance that your product or service has excellent quality and value. The fact that your clients are willing to provide the testimonial shows you have exceeded their expectations. This encourages the person to move deeper into the sales process.

Sales Professional:

It helps deepen the relationship between the sales professional and the person giving the testimonial. When a person puts in writing that you and your product/service are superior, it has a positive effect on the person's subconscious. In essence it helps program that person's subconscious mind to view you in a positive manner.

Sales Leadership:

All quality sales leaders are looking for ways to promote their team. Providing powerful testimonials to the marketing and senior company leadership is a good way to get their team the recognition they deserve. Having a team that is known for exceeding the expectations is the type of reputation that brings additional opportunities.

The sales professional knows how to create ways that everyone wins. Testimonials are a powerful win for everyone.

Tip #78

Don't talk bad about your competition.

You will never win by talking bad about your competitors. Refuse to engage in negative comments, even if your client asks you your opinion. Always reposition the conversation to focus on the positives of your company, your products and your services offered.

Tip #79

Make sure your work week includes two half days.

Yes, you read that right. Make sure your work week includes two half days! Here is the catch. There are 24 hours in a day. If you work a half day that means you would work 12 hours. By increasing your work day by 4 hours (assuming you work an 8 hour day) twice a week you will have gained 8 hours a week of production time. When you do that every month you increase your production time by 32 hours a month. Over the course of a year that is 384 extra production hours. That equates to approximately two and a half extra months of production time a year!

That simple formula is how you can increase your time to increase your income. Shift your paperwork and other nonessential activities you are doing during your peak selling hours to the off peak hours so you can increase your time engaged in high yielding activities. As explained in Tip # 45 it is imperative the majority of your time is invested in high yielding activities. Complete the paperwork and similar activities in the off peak hours.

How much more productive could you be if you had two and half extra months worth of production time? How much would you increase your income? Schedule two half days in your work week and you will be amazed at how you will accelerate your career and crush all your sales goals.

Tip #80

Tell the truth.

If you need any further explanation then you are in the wrong business!

Tip #81

Take responsibility for your actions.

One of the biggest ways to turn off clients and managers is to not own your actions. They are yours so take responsibility for them. Regardless if they are good or bad, take responsibility. The people who go through life making excuses and never taking responsibility for their actions are the ones who never realize the full measure of their opportunity.

Tip #82

Get rid of excuses.

This goes hand in hand with taking responsibility for your actions. So many times sales people want to make excuses for why they missed the sale. They become very creative and spend a lot of time convincing themselves it was beyond their control. The simple fact is excuses are negative and they only harm you, they never help you. So why would you purposely harm yourself? A negative excuse never produces a positive action! Find the explanation that leads to the opportunity for growth.

Excuse:

I missed the sale because I had to drive two hours the night before so I didn't have enough time to look over my materials.

Explanation:

I failed to prepare properly.

Explanation = Opportunity

I'm a professional and I will be prepared for my meetings.

From the example given what did the excuse produce? Nothing but more excuses. What did the explanation produce? It produced realization, responsibility, and the opportunity to learn and become better. Don't make excuses; make progress.

Tip #83

Ask yourself... Would I hire me based on my work ethic and performance?

This is a great way to give yourself a review of where you are right now. If you answer *No* to that question then make a list of the things you need to improve so you can answer *Yes*. Continue to ask yourself this question daily as a gauge of how productive you are. If you are honest with yourself there will be days you will have to answer *No*. Let that serve as motivation for the next day. You can make the choice to lie to yourself but remember you're not only hurting yourself you're hurting the people who love you and want you to succeed.

Tip #84

Look for time leaks.

If you're not producing as much as you would like, look for time leaks in your daily routine. Time is the most valuable asset you have and the professional knows you cannot let time leaks occur and stay productive. Some places for leaks are extended lunches, pointless conversations, non business emails (chain emails), office gossip, and the list goes on. All of these activities can potentially create time leaks that can drain hours away from your work week. Look for these leaks, correct them and you will become more productive. Rather than the time flowing away, you will begin to see the money flow to you.

Tip #85

Be pleasantly persistent.

If you have attended any sales meeting then you have heard that most sales are made after the fifth contact. However most sales people stop before they ever reach that number and move on to another lead. Be pleasantly persistent and continue to touch your future client adding value to them each time. By putting these future clients into your warming cycle (of your marketing plan) it will allow you to continue to touch them multiple times preparing the way for access and influence.

Tip #86

Understand the Pareto Principle.

The principle began in 1895 when Italian economist, Vilfredo Pareto observed that 80 percent of Italy's land was owned by 20 percent of the population. This caused people to begin to analyze other aspects of life. The more they looked the more they discovered that this 80/20 Rule seemed to apply to virtually everything. Today the Pareto Principle, or commonly referred to as the 80/20 Rule is an accepted business philosophy. In essence the rule states that the relationship between the input and the output is rarely, if ever balanced.

Here are some examples...

- 80 percent of your time will be invested in 20 percent of your clients.

- 20 percent of your clients will produce 80 percent of your income.

- 20 percent of your daily activities out produce the other 80 percent.

The list is endless but you get the idea. Remember the 80/20 is a guideline. It could be 70/30 or 85/15 the point is that a small amount of something is responsible for the majority of results. Find your 80/20 Rule in your business and allocate the resources to the proper area for increased success.

Tip #87

Counter Parkinson's Law.

We have all experienced the effects of a phenomenon known as Parkinson's Law. Parkinson's Law states that…

Work expands to fill the time allotted for it.

If we don't establish firm deadlines for ourselves and others, then we will continue to expand the work and put it off.   Successful sales people realize they must be able to counter Parkinson's Law to be effective. The first step is awareness, the second step is to use your time management system.

Tip #88

They are your clients not your Buds, Big Guys, Sweeties, or Pals.

We have all experienced the "sales guy" who loves to call everyone "Bud". They create these catch all names because they are lazy and ill prepared. I find it to be the mark of the amateur sales person. When they use these names what they are saying is that they aren't interested in the client only in the client's money. This is one of the fastest ways to turn off a perspective client. Use their name and build the relationship.

Tip #89

It's a presentation not a pitch.

Years ago sales people were taught to "pitch" their products. That meant to throw it out there and see if someone would hit it. Not only does it set the wrong mental picture of what you should be doing, it's a terrible strategy. The professional sales person uses a superior strategy that encompasses all the resources (marketing, excellent client service, referrals and a great product) to create an opportunity to be successful.

Pitch = Desperation

Presentation = Preparation

Your presentation is a professional representation of your company, product, service, and yourself. Leave the pitching to the amateurs and prepare a well planned and purposed presentation. Deliver it with precision of a professional and you will see your sales increase.

Tip #90

Use the waiter approach to client service.

The thing that makes a dining experience great is the service. We have all had an average meal but the service was so incredible that we go back. We have experienced the opposite where the meal was good but the service was so bad we would never go back. What was the real difference? It was the service.

What makes a great waiter? It's the one who is professional, friendly, provides quality suggestions when you are ordering, takes the time to answer your questions, accurately takes your order, makes sure your order is prepared correctly, allows you to enjoy the conversation with your guests with minimal interruptions, and fills your glass before it ever gets empty. This is the same approach to client service we need to have. Always being there for your client when they need something and giving them the space to enjoy the product. Look for ways to predict what they need and fill your client's glass before it gets empty.

Tip #91

Leverage social media.

Social media has the potential to connect you with an unlimited amount of people with little effort. There are many theories about the proper way to use social media, however, one thing is for sure it is a powerful tool. At a minimum you should have a professional online presence. One should be aware there is a difference between having a personal presence and a professional presence. Remember this is an area to connect, market and network with others. Be sure to keep your comments and photos professional understanding the purpose for your online presence is to create business not friends.

Tip #92

Don't work with bad clients.

Yes, there is such a thing. One of the hardest lessons for sales people to learn is to not work with bad clients. If you have a bad client; fire them! You are a professional and you deserve to work with the best. I have had my share of bad clients over the years just their name uttered in my presence caused my blood pressure to rise. They were hard to work with and never paid their bills on time. They were not respectful of my time and waited to the last minute to communicate on important topics. When I made the decision I was going to fire my bad clients I turned a corner in my career. I went from the feeling of not having control to being empowered. As a result I have become more selective in the clients I work with and my income has increased as well.

Bad clients take energy away from you and increase your exposure to negative comments. Don't work with them. Leave them for the amateur sales person; you're a professional.

Tip #93

Don't leave without confirming the next step.

The professional sales person always knows the next step of the sales process. They work to ensure they are moving the relationship to that step. Regardless if it's a sale or a follow up appointment know what it is and work to confirm it. You should never leave an appointment without confirming the next step. Every time you leave an appointment without clearly confirming the next step you have decreased the odds that you will be successful in opening the sale. So know what you need to happen, confirm it and increase your success rate.

Tip #94

Find a product or service that fills your life purpose.

Selling a product/service that helps fill your personal life purpose is perhaps the best way to a fulfilling sales career. Today most people live their life with reason. Reason is the *what you do to exist*. Their sales career is based on reason and they will represent any product or company that they feel like they can make the most money with. This can be exhausting and it leads to increased burnout and leaves you feeling less than fulfilled. Reason operates in the mind.

Purpose is the *why you exist*. It operates in your heart and those who successfully find a product or company that aligns with their purpose, experience a more rewarding career. If your purpose is to help parents who have a sick child then you need to find a product or service that helps you fulfill that purpose. Perhaps it is working with a nonprofit organization that needs a professional sales person to gain financial support for the organization. It could be selling a product that helps the physicians care for those children. The possibilities are limitless. The key is to find your purpose and let your sales career help you fill it.

Tip #95

Make a quality first impression.

It's common knowledge that people are constantly making judgments based on what they are observing. These judgments are the basis for determining whether they tune you in or tune you out. Most experts believe first impressions are created within the first ten to fifteen seconds of contact. The two largest contributors to first impressions are appearance and communication. Appearance is more than just how you look, it's how you carry yourself. Do you stand up straight or do you slouch? Do you display confidence or do you project arrogance? Communication is more than just words. It's the tone of the words as well as the body language we display. The sales professional understands the importance of first impressions and carries themselves in a manner to ensure they make a quality one.

Tip #96

Examine your wants, needs, and desires to inspire your actions.

We all have wants, needs and desires that if strong enough will motivate and inspire us to action. Often times we fail to properly use this internal system to our advantage. Perhaps you don't feel like you deserve the kind of success others have. Or you feel guilty for wanting so much. There are many factors that derail this powerful internal system from properly working for us. When you fully explore your wants, needs, and desires giving yourself permission, free from guilt, to experience these things you will have engaged this internal system and it will create action.

Tip #97

Research your future clients before your appointment.

Do some research to find out as much as you can about your client and their company. It is unwise to disclose all the information you know about them. However, most clients are impressed when you ask a question about a particular topic or item that they haven't mentioned.

This research can be completed in less than ten minutes in most cases with a quick search of the internet. The time you invest getting to know your client prior to your meeting will serve you well as you move through the sales process.

Tip #98

Prescribe the medication only after examination.

Find out what problem, desire, need, or want the client has and see how your product/service can solve that issue to fit your client. Amateur sales people have a product and try to fit the client into the product. This would be the equivalent to seeing a doctor, making some small talk, and then he/she prescribing a random medication and never once asks you about your symptoms. You wouldn't have much confidence or trust in that doctor would you? Why? Because they didn't take the time to properly examine and diagnose your problem. They prescribed the medication without basing it on your facts.

Same is true with our sales. Take the time to diagnosis the client and then prescribe the best product or service that will solve the issue.

Tip #99

Leverage technology.

Technology plays an important role in any business today. However there are those who merely use technology and fail to properly leverage it. Just as with anything there must be a proper balance. Too much technology and not enough personal interaction can leave your clients feeling unappreciated and under served. The key is to understand the areas you can let technology deliver the client service and when you personally need to deliver the service. Predetermine those areas that you will use technology and the areas you personally will be involved in. This is the best way to ensure that you don't abuse the technology but are leveraging it to your advantage.

Tip #100

Good is never good enough.

Why settle for being good at something when you can achieve greatness. Do you want to be known for being a good father or mother or would you strive to become a great one? Being good will get you by and you will have a good life. I chose to pursue greatness at everything I do because I don't want a good life, I want a great life! The same is true with your sales career. Do you want to earn a good living or a great living? Do you want to be introduced as a good sales person or a great sales person? The choice is yours. Your thoughts, actions, and commitment will determine your success.

Tip #101

Use plaques to recognize your clients.

This is one of the easiest and most cost effective ways that will allow you to accomplish multiple objectives with one program. Here is how the program works…

For example if you are selling a piece of equipment to a factory. The factory has multiple purchasing motivators but generally they always include,

1.   Increase production

2.   Increased safety

3.   Reduce production costs

After you have opened the deal and the equipment is delivered you deliver a plaque to the appropriate person. An example of the wording on the plaque would be…

Presented to

ABC Manufacturing

In recognition of your commitment to

Safety

and

Continued Production Excellence.

Presented by:

Your Company Name

(The date)

Plaques are powerful. They produce pride and are always hung in high profile places for others to see. They serve a number of benefits, listed below are a few.

The benefit to your client

1. They have an outside source that is saying they are committed to safety. Safety for manufactures is always a concern. Being able to hang a plaque in the lobby that recognizes their commitment to safety produces positive feelings.

2. It tells everyone who sees it that they are committed to production excellence. Perhaps it is a perspective client of theirs that comes to their office and sees this. It gives them additional credibility that they are doing excellent work.

The benefit to you and your company

1. It reinforces that your product or service is providing safety and allowing for their continued production excellence.

2. It serves as a marketing piece for your company when their colleagues visit.

3. Serves as a notice to other sales people that you have a relationship with them and this can be a powerful psychological tool that works against them.

4. There is the strong possibility that someone unrelated to your industry will see the plaque and use it as an ice breaker for their presentation. This reinforces the relationship with your company by other sources mentioning the benefits listed on the plaque.

It is worth noting the more unique the plaque is, the better the chances of others commenting on it are. Always list the human element on the plaque first. In this example safety has the strongest human element so it was listed first followed by the business element of continued production excellence. Regardless of your industry look for ways to appreciate your clients.

Tip #102

Remember everyone is selling something. What are you buying?

Everyone is selling something. Perhaps it's an excuse not to own your product or service. It could be an image a person wants to convey to you. Regardless, everyone has something to sell. The most common things we buy require no money. They are purchased with our thoughts, ideas, and feelings. So be careful and aware of what you are buying and make sure it is positive and helps to improve your life. Avoid people who are selling negativity and excuses, this will cost you opportunities, happiness, and rob you of your valuable asset, time.

Tip #103

Exceed the expectations of others on the sales team.

Expectations are the minimum. Commit to doing more than the expectations. This will serve you well with your clients and your sales mangers. Do you want to be known for meeting the minimum expectations or exceeding them?

Opportunities are multiplied for those who exceed the expectations. Commit to exceeding your teams expectations, and you will have committed to a successful sales career.

Conclusion

This book contains not only the proven sales tips that you will accelerate your career, but also a powerful sales philosophy. The philosophy is woven into these sales tips like a fine tapestry; revealing itself to you as you apply these sales tips. The more application, the more it reveals itself to you. Like a partnership it is developing you and you are developing it.

In Tip # 50 we discussed the need to always exceed the expectations of your clients. It was my aim to have done that with this book by adding value to your life and your career. To help illustrate that point and to ensure that I have exceeded your expectations, I have included ten bonus tips that will take you from 103 Proven Sales Tips to 113 Proven Sales Tips! It's been a privilege to serve you.

Bonus Tip #104

Stop Cold Calling!

Stop cold calling! We are using terms and strategies that were adopted in the 1920's. The premise is the call is unsolicited and you are dropping by unannounced. There are a few things wrong with this approach. People and business owners are busy. The way we interact on a social level has changed. Years ago it might have been acceptable to drop in on a person at their home or business unexpected, today it is not. Most of us don't even like our friends dropping by unexpected. One of the largest problems any sales organization faces with its sales force is call reluctance. Many great business minds have struggled to find a solution to this problem. Organizations spend millions of dollars each year with incentive trips and special programs all in an attempt to counter it. The simple truth to the problem is the approach to the method of selling.

I'm not claiming to have the solution to solve a century or older problem; however, I will provide a few thoughts that perhaps will generate ideas and additional strategies that can help you personally combat this death sentence for your career.

The most powerful tool you have is your mind. In your mind lies your attitude, your self-worth, your thoughts, hopes, beliefs, desires, and your fears. I suggested to you in Tip # 68 rejection is not personal. Yet we know the fear of rejection is a dominate fear for most people. So when you hear the word cold call over and over again you start to associate that with a negative emotion or fear. The word *cold* in context of a drink on a hot day it's a positive thing, however, in the sales world the mental image the subconscious strikes is different picture and felling. Cold for some can spark emotions of loneliness, failure, and of isolation. So when we know we have a day filled of *cold calling* what happens? We naturally tend to be reluctant.

When I was a police officer I noticed every time I used the word ticket, I could see the driver's blood pressure rise. The word ticket immediately translated in their mind to; this is going to cost money, my car insurance is going up, and I will need to go to court, among many other things. All the emotions were negative. I started to search for a neutral word to use. I began to use the word citation. The simple adjustment in the word immediately changed things. It didn't spark any negative thoughts, in fact, I began to have people thank me for writing them a citation. I began to teach all our officers to use the word citation and something amazing happened. Our complaints went down and our officers became friendlier. Just changing one word made a huge difference.

As I entered the business world I saw that many organizations had yet to apply this basic principle to their business. They were teaching the cold call and to fear the gate keeper, they wondered why they had such a high turnover in sales personnel. The fact was that unintentionally they were scaring them off. They were torturing these people psychologically.

I have coached and counseled countless sales people who would stay up at night sick to their stomachs because of the thought of cold calling and the gate keeper. Clearly, this is not the way to have a long and successful career in selling or to build a profitable organization. In Tip #40 we discussed thinking of the gate keeper as an information ambassador not the enemy. In this tip I'm advising you to replace the cold call with the marketing touch. This is a neutral word and as I explained in Tip# 18 it generally takes multiple marketing touches to complete the sale. So know that marketing touches are a good thing. This is all part of your larger marketing concept we have discussed throughout the book. When you make the transition from prospecting filled with cold calling, to a marketing plan filled with marketing touches, you have made the mental shift into a system of strategy, tactics, and techniques.

Bonus Tip #105

Invest time with yourself and the ones you love.

In life we have the choice to either be healthy or not. This health is not just physical health but the health that comes from having balance in one's life. This is the balance of your personal life as well as your professional life. Too often we get consumed with the sale and start to neglect ourselves and family, this leads to an unhealthy and unbalanced life. If not corrected this begins to create diseased relationships which severely affects all aspects of your life. Invest time with your loved ones and yourself. Seek health and balance between your personal and professional life. Make it a priority to have health in these key power areas; mental, physical, spiritual, and emotional. One cannot achieve this type of health by neglecting any area. Invest time in your health and you will see your career will become healthier as well.

Bonus Tip #106

It's not what if? It's when then.

What if? We have all heard this approach used to sell an idea or product. In most cases we are so desensitized to the question that it has almost no impact on us. From the time we are children we have been posed the "what if" question. Begin to use the phrase When/Then.

When you retire, Then what will you do?

When the market goes up, Then you'll be in a great position.

The When/Then combination encourages action. It can be positioned in virtually any market.

Bonus Tip #107

Stop trying.

We have all heard the new sales person say "I'll give it a try and see what happens." What do you think happens? Nothing in most cases, trying doesn't equal a commitment. We must be determined to make it happen. Become determined to make it work as if there was not any other option. We are all blessed with the gift of determination when we are born. Through our life experiences most people build layers of fear and doubt over this powerful gift. The sales professional knows trying will never lead to the success they demand. It is through their gift of determination that they succeed. Stop trying and start doing!

Bonus Tip #108

Failure is your friend.

Society has been selling people the idea that failure is the opposite of success, that failure is the mark of the fool, failure will make you a loser, and that if you are to become successful you must avoid failure. In essence they are saying it is better to have never started your journey if it doesn't end with what society views as success. The truth of the matter is failure is your friend. In fact, failure is the prerequisite to success. The wrong ideas about failure exist, truly there is only one way you ever fail and that is to give up. Everything else is part of the success journey. Most successes are a series of "failures" that have lead to the break through moment. Know that you are on a journey, and the journey will be marked with highs and lows, with many "failures" and many successes. Embrace "failure" as part of the success journey. Knowing that right around the corner is everything you deserve and have worked to achieve.

Bonus Tip #109

Stop procrastinating.

Procrastination is one of the largest threats to the sales person. Procrastination wears many disguises to keep you from knowing its true identity. It affects both personal and business lives. Procrastination is responsible for many missed opportunities. If you are not achieving the success you want, take an honest look to see if you are procrastinating in areas you could be excelling in. Value time, invest it wisely, and commit today to procrastinate no more.

Bonus Tip #110

Hunting vs. Farming

There are two types of sales: Hunting and Farming. They are both essential to a healthy and balanced business and career. However, some personality types will be more attracted to one or the other; the professional knows it is wise to do both.

Hunting:

This is an aggressive and proactive approach to developing business quickly. Hunting produces quick results and typically requires a high energy level professional.

Farming:

This is a less aggressive approach but still requires the professional to be proactive. Typically, farming will be a slower process and is a much more controlled environment. Farming follows a predictable system that generally can be replicated.

Farming can be classified into two categories; First Year Crop and Reoccurring Crops.

- **First Year Crop:**

These are clients you cultivated a relationship with over the course of some time (Warming Cycle). It was that cultivation that allowed the business to develop into your first sell.

- **Reoccurring Crop:**

This is where all your clients should end up, regardless if they were acquired through hunting or first year crop farming. The idea is you will cultivate the client to continue to produce a financial crop for you season after season.

When you approach the client relationship with the mentality that you are planting seeds for your future crop the task of providing excellent client service becomes an essential part of your marketing plan. Truly there are many ways to cultivate your clients, just as the farmer does more than plant; you should too. Take the time to water, to make sure the soil is right to sustain growth, but beyond that, make sure the seeds you are planting are the seeds that are going to produce the correct crop you need at harvest.

Bonus Tip #111

Be organized.

Part of being prepared is being organized. Organization is a skill that most of us have to learn. The professionals know if they are to maximize opportunities they must be organized and prepared for them. Disorganization slows business growth and personal development. Organization is part of becoming a high performance professional. Commit to organization.

Bonus Tip #112

Remain Positive
and Focused.

A career in sales can take its toll even on the strongest of professionals. Stay positive and focused on reaching your goals. Reward yourself with positive activities you enjoy and that will keep you on your success track. Avoid negative people and activities. Being engaged in negative thoughts will only slow your career and ultimately derail the success train that you are on. Remain positive and focused on your career.

Bonus Tip #113

Serve others.

Truly there is only one way to become successful in this life and that is to serve others. Seek to add value to people regardless of who they are. Serving people with a sincere heart and honest intentions will do more for your career than any other thing. Spend a life-time serving others and you will have found a life that was worth living. Success is defined in many ways by many different people, however, the book of Matthew 23:11 Jesus said, "The person who is greatest among you will be your servant." Serving others is important and it is what makes a person successful.

Final Thoughts

Years ago I was taught a valuable lesson from Eric Enck whose company Enck Consulting is on the leading edge of practical self-defense skills for women and children. Eric is a fifth-degree black belt in Wado Ryu Karate and holds numerous belts in other martial arts disciplines. Eric had just started working with me to develop more power in my punches and kicks and one day it happened. While he was holding the bag that I was punching, he unlocked the door for me. What he said changed my life forever. Eric looked at me and said, "You're trying to punch the bag." I had no idea what he was trying to convey to me, and he must have figured that out by the look on my face. He said, "You need to punch through the bag. You are limiting your power because you're trying to punch the bag. The power comes not from hitting the target, but from punching through the target, driving completely through it." The door swung wide open for me, not just to create power in my punch but to create power in my life. The power to reach past my potential and to achieve the highest levels in all aspects of my life.

So often we just look at the target and think if we touch it, then we have succeeded. When the reality is the power comes not from the touch, but the drive of going through it. We shouldn't focus on just reaching our potential—we need to focus on reaching past our potential.

Perhaps you have been in the same position I have been, just trying to hit the target and wondering why you feel so powerless. My hope is the door has been unlocked for you to achieve greatness. To look beyond what you can see right now, and to reach past your potential.

Selling, like life, is about people. It's about relating and being related to. We often hear that selling is a numbers game and that is true. The number is *one*. There is only one of you, and you are the only *one* that can choose success for yourself. You are the only *one* that will embrace the thought that you are in control of your life and that excuses are no longer part of it. Rather than excuses, you seek the true explanations that lead to opportunities for your growth. You are the *one* that puts into practice a goal reaching plan and enjoys the success from reaching your goals. You are the *one* that sells in your purpose, thus allowing you to fulfill your life purpose. It is a numbers game; I believe that, we just need to focus on the number *one*.

My desire for you is to live the life that you were meant to live. A life filled with purpose, health and determination. A life that you reach past your potential!

Let's connect

-Justin

About the Author

Justin lives in middle Tennessee with his wife and three children. He is recognized as an expert in sales, leadership and personal development. His success has put him on a virtual platform with the leading experts such as Anthony Robbins, Brain Tracy, and Zig Ziglar.

Justin's diverse professional career in politics, law enforcement, and business allows him to bring fresh perspectives to the discussion. His unique ability to connect with an audience has made him a sought after speaker. His workshops and seminars on Sales, Leadership, and Personal Development are inspiring a new generation to reach past their potential.

Connect with Justin at,

www.JustinHammonds.com

For Free Bonus
Videos Visit

www.103ProvenSalesTips.com

www.ingramcontent.com/pod-product-compliance
Lightning Source LLC
Chambersburg PA
CBHW060025210326
41520CB00009B/1009